D0513491

bodymatters

jamal is
overweight
janine amos

CHERRYTREE BOOKS

bodymatters
Kate Smokes Cigarettes
Jon Drinks Alcohol
Why Won't Kim Eat?
Is Helen Pregnant?
Alex Does Drugs
Jamal is Overweight

A Cherrytree Book

First published 2002
by Cherrytree Press
327 High Street
Slough
Berkshire
SL1 1TX

© Evans Brothers Limited 2002

British Library Cataloguing in Publication Data

Amos, Janine
Jamal is overweight. - (Bodymatters)
1. Obesity - Juvenile literature
I. Title
616.3'98

ISBN 1842341111

Printed in Hong Kong by Wing King Tong Co Ltd

Acknowledgements
Planning and production: Discovery Books
Editor: Patience Coster
Photo research: Rachel Tisdale
Photographer: David Simson
Designer: Keith Williams
Artwork: Fred van Deelen
Consultant: Dr Gillian Rice

**All the characters appearing in this book
are played by models.**

Picture acknowledgements
The publisher would like to thank the
following for permission to reproduce
their pictures: Science Photo Library 23
(John Bavosi); Corbis 27 (Brian Leng).

jamal is
overweight

contents

Jamal's class is choosing sides for football.

Conrad and the new boy Tim are team captains. They get to choose the players.

Tim looks across at Jamal.

'Don't choose him – he isn't fast,' someone hisses.

Jamal goes red. He stares down at his boots. Tim takes Ollie instead, and Jamal trudges over to Conrad's team.

'Where shall we put you?' wonders Conrad, frowning at Jamal. 'You might be OK in goal.'

All through the lesson Jamal stands in goal. He feels the wind blowing down the back of his sweatshirt. He wishes he was indoors in the warm. Jamal lets two goals in – and Conrad's team loses.

Jamal walks home with his friend Sally. He tells her how much he hates football. As they pass the corner shop he smells doughnuts. Delicious!

'Just what I need!' says Jamal. 'Come on!'

'I'd better not,' Sally tells him. 'I won't eat my supper.'

Jamal buys two jam

A question of taste

Foods contain many chemicals. When you eat, tiny bumps on your tongue called taste buds pick up these chemicals. The tip of your tongue picks up sweet tastes. Behind this are the taste buds that pick up saltiness, while those at the sides pick up sour tastes. Those at the back detect bitterness. The taste buds send this information to your brain.

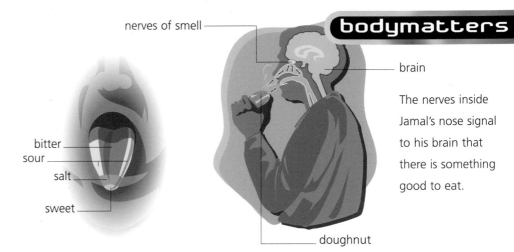

nerves of smell

bitter
sour
salt
sweet

brain

The nerves inside Jamal's nose signal to his brain that there is something good to eat.

doughnut

weight and fitness

Food and us

Everybody needs food. We eat food to give our bodies energy, to help us grow and to keep us healthy.

We enjoy eating too. As Jamal smells the doughnuts, nerves inside his nose send messages to his brain telling him there's something good to eat. Jamal's brain sends signals to his mouth and stomach, preparing them for the food to come. His mouth waters and his stomach begins to make juices ready to work on the first doughnut, before it even enters his mouth.

doughnuts and eats them both.

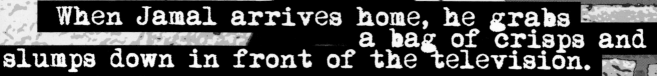

When Jamal arrives home, he grabs a bag of crisps and slumps down in front of the television.

As he watches the programme, his hand dips in and out of the bag until all the crisps are gone. He washes them down with a fizzy drink.

When Jamal's mum, Nura, gets in from work, they have their evening meal.

'Tonight it's-a pasta!' declares Jamal's dad, Ahmed, in his best Italian accent. 'With-a special creamy sauce!'

Jamal's dad enjoys cooking – and Jamal and Nura enjoy eating what Ahmed cooks. Later, Jamal goes to his room to play on his computer. On the way he passes the kitchen and sees Nura with the cookie jar.

'Help yourself,' she offers, 'they're your favourite chocolate chip.'

Jamal takes a handful.

enjoying food

Food inside

When Jamal eats his supper, his teeth grind and mix the food together so he can swallow it. The juices in his mouth make the food easier to swallow. It then passes down into his stomach. Here, stomach juices are added to the food as it is mashed and squeezed into a kind of paste.

A few hours later, the food moves into a long tube lower down inside Jamal's body called the small intestine.

Here, chemicals produced by his body soak into the food and break it down into tiny pieces, called molecules. This whole process takes about two days. The molecules of food are so tiny that they can pass through the walls of Jamal's small intestine and into his blood.

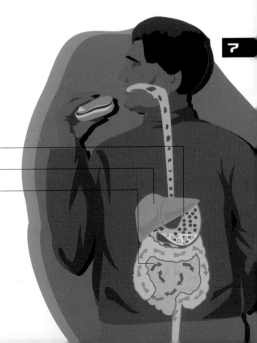

stomach

liver

small intestine

Inside Jamal's small intestine the food is broken down into tiny pieces so that his body can use it.

There are some parts of the food his body can't use. These pass out as waste when he goes to the toilet. This process is called digestion.

7

At the weekend, Jamal relaxes with his mum and dad.

They share some butterscotch popcorn while watching TV. Even though it's only halfway through the afternoon, Jamal feels very sleepy. When the doorbell rings he pads to answer it, yawning.

It's Mick and Ali from the next street.

'We're on a bike ride,' says Mick. 'We're going along the cycle track out of town. D'you want to come?'

Jamal yawns again. 'No thanks, we've got a video. See you!'

He watches the boys speed off. Then he trails back to the sitting room, picking up a packet of crisps on the way.

'Fancy a TV supper tonight?' asks Ahmed. 'How about fish and chips?'

'Yes please,' nods Jamal.

8

the food we eat

The food we eat is made up of different parts called nutrients. Some foods contain more nutrients than others. We need a mix of nutrients to keep our bodies healthy, help us grow and give us energy.

Most of our energy comes from carbohydrates, which are the sugars and starches in foods. Fats also provide energy and keep us warm. Proteins are especially important for young people whose bodies are still growing.

They help the body to grow, and to repair itself if it is damaged. Vitamins and minerals help keep our bodies healthy.

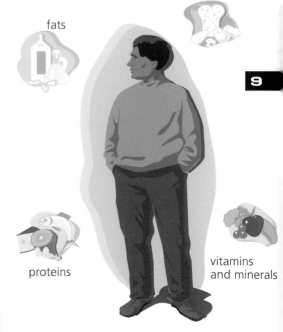

fats

carbohydrates

proteins

vitamins and minerals

9

Snack attack!
Like many people, Jamal enjoys eating foods like crisps and biscuits. They contain mostly sugars and fats – far more than his body needs – and not many other nutrients.

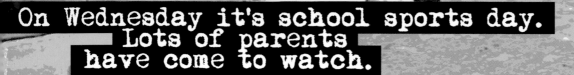

On Wednesday it's school sports day. Lots of parents have come to watch.

Jamal feels sick and scared. He hates running in front of everyone. He hates sports day.

Everyone in the class has to line up waiting for their turn to race. Jamal's heart is thumping in his chest. He knows he'll come last, as usual. He imagines struggling down the track with everyone else ahead of him.

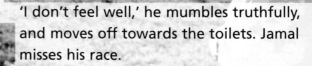

'I don't feel well,' he mumbles truthfully, and moves off towards the toilets. Jamal misses his race.

At home time Sally sees him sitting on his own, looking miserable.

'Where did you disappear to?' she asks. 'Why didn't you run?'

'Running's a waste of time,' says Jamal fiercely. 'I'll only look stupid in front of everyone.'

Sally is quiet for a while. 'Maybe you'd feel better about yourself if you were a bit fitter,' she says gently.

'You mean go on a diet?' asks Jamal, looking up.

'Perhaps I should

10

energy

The energy producers

All living things are made up of cells. To do its work, every cell in the body must produce energy. This energy comes from food.

Jamal's blood carries food molecules to his cells through tiny tubes called capillaries.

**give it a try,'
he says, gloomily.**

The cells contain parts called mitochondria, which act like power generators. They use the food molecules as fuel, burning them up to produce energy. But Jamal's body isn't using all the food he's taking in. His blood contains more food than his mitochondria can burn. His body will store what is left – as fat.

A store for survival

The body stores fat to guard against starvation. In ancient times, when food was regularly hard to get, a store of fat was essential for survival. Today, most people in the West never have to go without food. But their bodies still operate as if they might.

The next morning, Jamal wakes up early.
He hunts for the bathroom scales.

He finds them at the back of a cupboard, covered with fluff. Jamal weighs himself and groans.

At breakfast, Jamal eats one slice of toast. His stomach starts rumbling midway through the morning. But at lunchtime he only eats half his packed lunch. Jamal is taking his diet seriously.

All week it's the same. Jamal eats no cookies, crisps or chocolate. He asks for small tuna salads instead of burger and chips. His mum and dad raise their eyebrows, but they don't say a word.

On Monday morning, Jamal steps
on to the scales again

dieting

Emergency fuel

Jamal has lost three kilos in a short time. The diet is a shock to his body. Jamal is using energy every minute – to think, move around, even to sleep. At the moment he isn't eating enough food to give him the energy he needs. But Jamal's body won't give up his fat stores straight away. It has an emergency supply of fuel to use up first. This is a type of sugar called glucose, which will be released from Jamal's liver.

Glucose is quickly used up by the mitochondria. As the glucose is released, so are large amounts of water. Almost all the weight that Jamal has lost is made up of glucose and water. His fat stores have not been used.

**and smiles.
He's losing weight.**

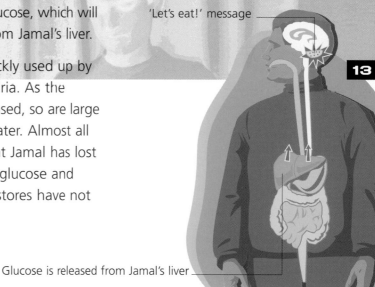

When Jamal's glucose supplies are low, his brain sends out a 'Let's eat!' message

Glucose is released from Jamal's liver

13

A few days later, Jamal sits in his classroom and sighs.

The pages of sums swim before his eyes. He's thinking about a delicious baklava pastry, soaked in honey syrup. He imagines it in front of him, warm from the oven. His mouth waters.

'Jamal!' shouts the teacher, making Jamal jump. 'Answer, please, we haven't got all day!'

Jamal looks down at his book and tries to remember the question.

Jamal isn't happy on his diet. He feels weak and he can't concentrate on anything for very long.

He has a headache, he's tired

Fat stores

By now, Jamal's glucose stores are running out. It's time to burn some stored fat. But Jamal's body wants to keep that fat store for as long as possible. His fat cells send a signal for help to his brain. In reply, Jamal's brain works harder to urge him to eat.

At the same time, brain signals instruct the mitochondria to burn fuel more slowly. Each bite of food Jamal swallows will now last longer inside him. His whole body is slowing down. And fat is much lighter than glucose and water. It will take Jamal about four more weeks of hard dieting to lose another three kilos.

slowing down

all the time, and he just can't stop thinking about food.

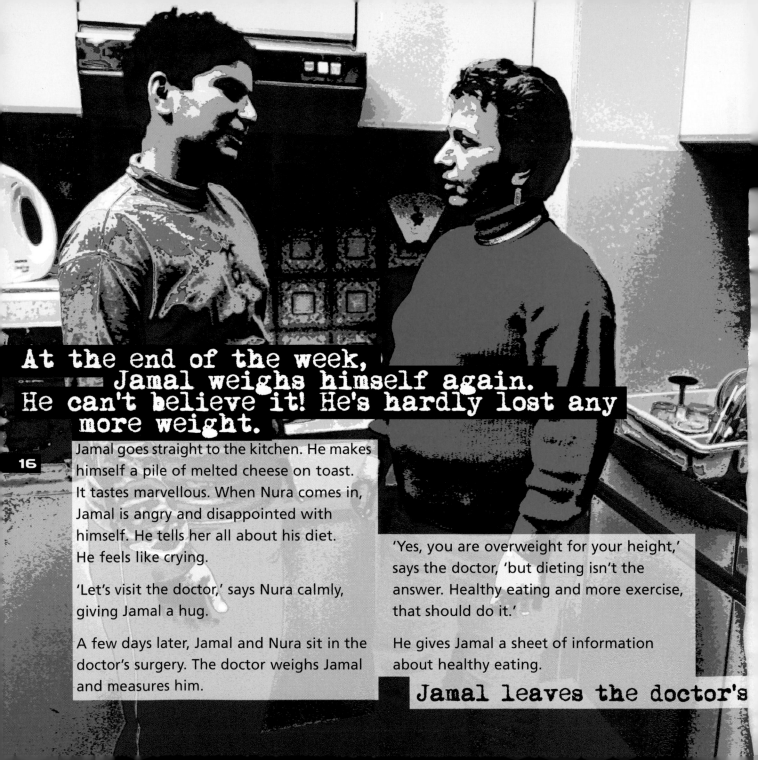

At the end of the week, Jamal weighs himself again. He can't believe it! He's hardly lost any more weight.

Jamal goes straight to the kitchen. He makes himself a pile of melted cheese on toast. It tastes marvellous. When Nura comes in, Jamal is angry and disappointed with himself. He tells her all about his diet. He feels like crying.

'Let's visit the doctor,' says Nura calmly, giving Jamal a hug.

A few days later, Jamal and Nura sit in the doctor's surgery. The doctor weighs Jamal and measures him.

'Yes, you are overweight for your height,' says the doctor, 'but dieting isn't the answer. Healthy eating and more exercise, that should do it.'

He gives Jamal a sheet of information about healthy eating.

Jamal leaves the doctor's

healthy eating

Eating well

What does the doctor mean by healthy eating? He gives Jamal a sheet of information about food. It shows the amounts we need to eat of each group of foods.

Pasta, bread, rice and potatoes

Wholemeal bread and pasta and brown rice are especially good. They contain fibre, which helps the body move food through the intestines.

Fruit and vegetables

Eat as many kinds as you can. Try to eat five portions a day to make sure you're getting the vitamins and minerals your body needs.

Proteins

Proteins include meat, fish, pulses, nuts, beans and eggs. You should eat about two servings a day.

Dairy foods

These include milk, cheese, and yogurt. You should eat about two or three servings a day.

Fats and sugary foods

These include crisps, mayonnaise, ice cream, doughnuts, cookies, sweets, tinned fruit and fizzy drinks. Try to eat only small amounts of these. They are high in fat or sugar – often both! – and don't contain many other nutrients.

17

This shows the balance of foods we need to eat to stay healthy.

surgery feeling a bit more cheerful.

Back home, Jamal tells Ahmed what the doctor said.

He sticks the food chart on to the fridge door. Ahmed looks down at his own stomach.

'I think I could do with some exercise too,' he says. Then he goes to make a telephone call.

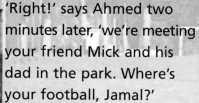

'Right!' says Ahmed two minutes later, 'we're meeting your friend Mick and his dad in the park. Where's your football, Jamal?'

Jamal groans, but he goes off to fetch it.

'I'm coming too,' says Nura suddenly. 'I'm not having you getting fit without me!'

Soon they're all in the park, running about after the ball. Jamal's face is bright red and he's sweating but he's having a great time.

'This is a laugh!' he thinks, puffing.

After a while, Jamal needs to stop. So does Nura.

'That's enough for our family for now,' she says. 'Our bodies aren't used to it. We'd better not do too much too soon!'

Ahmed agrees. 'We'll see

Moving muscle

When Jamal runs after the ball, his brain sends messages to his muscles to get them moving. As his muscles move, the mitochondria inside start to burn more energy to fuel the movements.

Suddenly Jamal's muscles need a lot more energy – at least sixty times more – than they did when he was resting. At last they need to use the energy that's locked away in Jamal's fat stores. Jamal's mitochondria can't work this fast, they just aren't used to it. And, because he hasn't used them much before, there aren't enough capillaries in Jamal's muscles to deliver the energy he now needs. After his first kickaround in the park, Jamal is exhausted.

Calories

Muscles need energy to work. Energy comes from the food we eat and is measured in units called calories. Everything Jamal eats contains calories, and everything he does uses them up. Any extra exercise Jamal takes will burn off more calories, including those stored as fat. If he's burning up more calories than he's taking in, he will lose weight.

exercise

19

you tomorrow, though!'
he calls out to the others.

the effects

The next morning, Jamal's body aches.

All day long he can feel pains in his arms and legs. When he gets home from school he wants to lie on the sofa. Nura feels the same.

'Come on, you two!' says Ahmed, grabbing the football. 'The more exercise you take, the easier it gets.'

Jamal groans.

When Jamal runs around again it does feel easier. He even scores a goal.

They play football in the park most evenings. Mick and his dad play too, and so does Ali. Sometimes there's a crowd. At weekends, Jamal and Ahmed go swimming. Sally is often there too.

These days, Jamal hardly has time to watch

# of exercise

Making a difference

Ahmed is right. The more exercise Jamal does, the more his body can cope with. The exercise he's taking is making changes to his body too.

New capillaries are growing in Jamal's muscles. They allow more energy to be carried to his muscles. Jamal is burning up all the food he's eating. He is also burning up the energy his body has stored as fat. Because he's eating plenty, he no longer feels hungry.

In Jamal's muscle cells, the mitochondria begin to divide so there are more of them. They can now produce much more energy than they could before.

television.

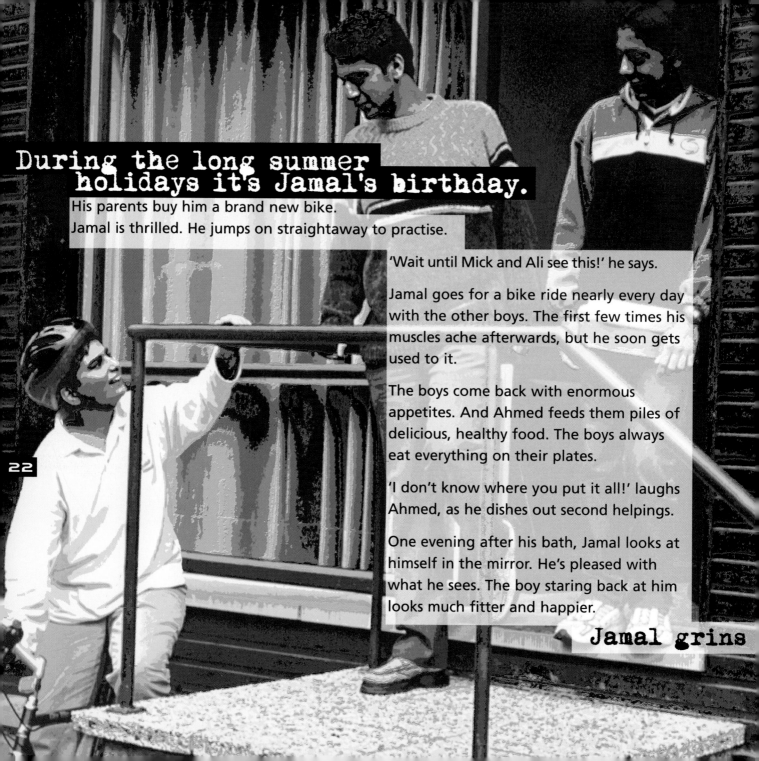

During the long summer holidays it's Jamal's birthday.

His parents buy him a brand new bike.
Jamal is thrilled. He jumps on straightaway to practise.

'Wait until Mick and Ali see this!' he says.

Jamal goes for a bike ride nearly every day with the other boys. The first few times his muscles ache afterwards, but he soon gets used to it.

The boys come back with enormous appetites. And Ahmed feeds them piles of delicious, healthy food. The boys always eat everything on their plates.

'I don't know where you put it all!' laughs Ahmed, as he dishes out second helpings.

One evening after his bath, Jamal looks at himself in the mirror. He's pleased with what he sees. The boy staring back at him looks much fitter and happier.

Jamal grins

Muscle power

Your body has hundreds of muscles with different jobs to do. Muscles in your stomach mash up your food. Muscles in your chest help you to breathe. The muscle called your heart pumps blood around your body. Some kinds of muscles allow you to make movements by pulling on the bones they are attached to. In order to work, muscles need plenty of nutrients from the food you eat and oxygen from the air you breathe.

Muscle-building

The more exercise Jamal does, the more energy his muscles burn – and the better they work. All the exercise is having a big effect on Jamal's body. More energy is reaching his muscles through the new capillaries. And there are lots more mitochondria to burn it up.

The fat stores in his body are disappearing from around his stomach and under his chin. The fat is taken to the places he needs it – to his muscles. Whenever Jamal wants to ride his bike, swim or play football, his body now has a supply of ready energy. Jamal's body is building muscle.

getting fitter

at his reflection.

The human skeleton is covered with muscles, which pull on the bones and enable the body to move.

One afternoon at the end of the holidays, Jamal is at the leisure centre with Sally.

The pool is quite quiet so there's plenty of space to swim.

'Look, there are Conrad and Ollie from school,' says Sally. 'We haven't seen them all summer.'

Sally and Jamal wave to the boys, who swim across. Soon they're all splashing about together. After a while, Conrad swims off, doing a powerful stroke. Suddenly, Jamal decides to join him. He pushes himself through the water and catches up easily. They swim up and down the pool, side by side.

When they stop to rest, Jamal shakes the water out of his ears and grins. He really enjoyed that swim.

Afterwards, Jamal and Sally cycle home together.

'How does it feel to be fit, then?' asks Sally, smiling.

'Great!' grins Jamal.

24

fit for life

Snacks

Not all the foods you like are bad for you! Snack foods can be healthy. Try some of these the next time you feel like snacking:

- peanut butter and crackers
- yogurt
- breakfast cereal (without a sugar coating or added sugar) and milk
- carrots
- raisins
- apples
- pitta bread and tuna
- bread sticks

It is worth taking regular exercise to help yourself keep fit and well. Try also to avoid eating the wrong foods. Although foods containing sugar may taste good, too much sugar is bad for you.

Too much sugar in your mouth causes problems for your teeth. Soft drinks, biscuits, cakes and sweets are high in sugar. But so are many tinned and packet foods, which are meant to be savoury. To find out exactly what you're eating, check the food labels on the packets – you may be surprised to see what they contain.

Eating healthily is important for your body, both inside and out.

A good, balanced diet will improve the way your body works. Your skin will be clearer and your hair shinier if you eat plenty of fruit and vegetables and avoid too many fatty foods and sweet drinks. Use the following as a checklist:

- eat plenty of fruit and vegetables
- eat plenty of potatoes, rice, pasta and bread (wholemeal kinds are best)
- eat a variety of foods
- don't have too many foods or drinks that contain a lot of fat or sugar
- enjoy eating!

a balanced diet

These are the kinds of foods that are healthy to eat. Try to include plenty of fruit and vegetables in your diet.

If you think you are overweight:

- Talk to an adult you trust

- Visit your doctor and ask for advice

- Take up some kind of exercise

- Eat more healthy foods and cut down on the sweet and fatty ones

- Eat when you're hungry (not when you're sad, angry or bored)

- Remember, small changes to your diet and lifestyle work best

As well as helping to burn off fat and build muscle, exercise has other good effects on your body.

The harder you make your body work, the faster your heart will pump to deliver nutrients and oxygen to your muscles. At the same time, your lungs are able to take in more oxygen from the air. You breathe faster and deeper. The extra exercise and increased oxygen improve the way your heart and muscles work. Like Jamal, your body will learn to cope with exercise more easily over time. You won't pant so much and your heart won't race. You'll be getting fit.

Exercise also lifts your mood. When you exercise, chemicals called endorphins are pumped into your bloodstream to give you a burst of well-being. Exercise is good for you – and it makes you feel good too.

Exercise-wise
Just fifteen minutes of exercise three times a day will make you fitter. If you're short of ideas for what to do, try some of these. (Remember – if you're out and about, it's safer to be with a friend):

On your own
skipping; skateboarding; trampolining; cycling; dancing; gymnastics; riding; self-defence classes; swimming; weight-lifting.

With a friend
running; orienteering; fast-walking; dog-walking; tennis; badminton; table tennis; basketball; frisbee; football; climbing.

With a crowd
any of the above, plus volleyball; softball; cricket.

(Always wear a helmet if you're travelling on wheels!)

action!

Exercise facts

- If you watch TV for two hours a day, in a year you'll see 20,000 messages encouraging you to eat!

- Many processed and 'fast foods' contain lots of sugar, salt and fat.

- Exercise can be addictive! Don't let it take up all your time – a little exercise every day is fine. Never exercise hard in very hot weather or if you aren't well.

- Small changes to your lifestyle will all add up to a fitter you. Try using stairs instead of escalators or walking to school with a friend some days instead of taking the bus.

glossary

calorie a unit of energy. Everything you eat contains calories and everything you do uses them up.

capilliary a very fine tube which carries blood in your body

carbohydrates the starches and sugars in food which give you energy

cell the smallest living part of you

endorphins chemicals produced in your brain which are released when you exercise. Endorphins dull pain and give a feeling of well-being.

fats nutrients that your body needs for energy, warmth and to help take in some kinds of vitamins

minerals nutrients that are taken up from the earth by plants and which enter the body as food

mitochondria parts of a cell which act as power generators, burning up food to produce energy

molecules tiny parts of a substance

nerves tiny cords which send messages between the brain and other parts of the body

nutrients chemicals found in food which the body needs in order to grow, keep healthy and to provide energy

oxygen a colourless gas that is in the air and which we need in order to live

proteins nutrients that the body needs in order to grow and repair itself

taste buds groups of cells on the tongue, which can tell whether a food is salty, sweet, bitter or sour

vitamins nutrients that your body needs in small amounts. There are thirteen vitamins.

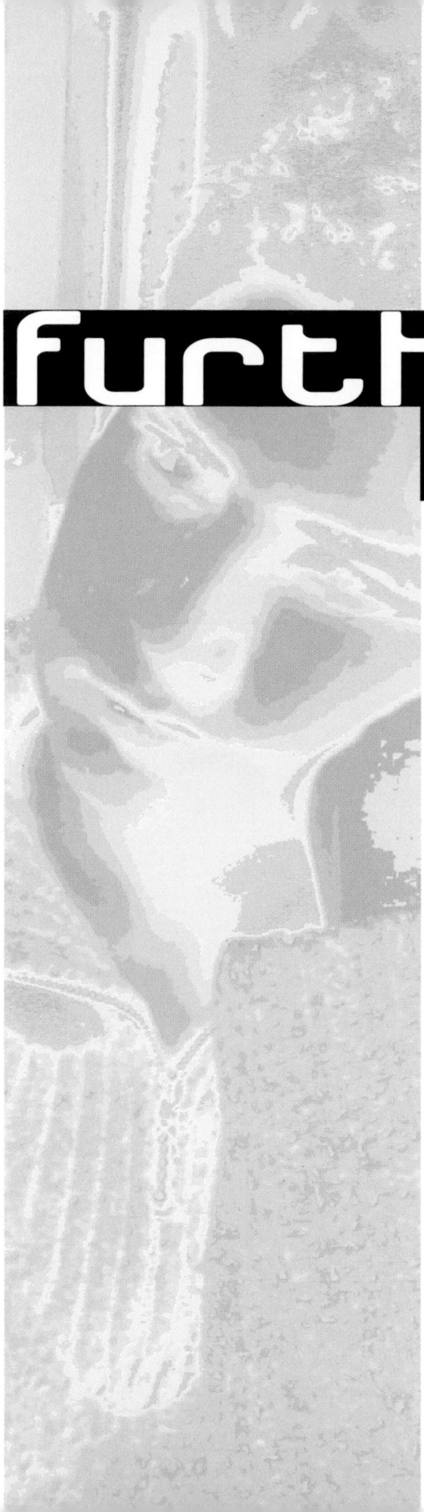

further information

Getting help

If you have a problem with your weight, there are people who can help. Talk to an adult you trust. Go to your doctor. You could also phone one of these offices. Sometimes the telephone lines are busy. If they are, don't give up – keep trying.

Kidscape

020 7730 3300

A national charity which can help children and young people if they are being bullied.

ChildLine

Freephone 0800 1111

websites

http://websrv01.kidshealth.org
http://www.nutrition.org.uk

31

index

The numbers in **bold** refer to illustrations.

32